T0208396

BRING LILIES

BRING LILIES

THE PATH TO AWAKENING

*Poems and Meditations
for the Journey*

Madeline Rowe

BALBOA.PRESS
A DIVISION OF HAY HOUSE

Balboa Press books may be ordered through booksellers or by contacting:

Balboa Press
A Division of Hay House
1663 Liberty Drive
Bloomington, IN 47403
www.balboapress.com
844-682-1282

Print information available on the last page.

ISBN: 979-8-7652-4782-2 (sc)
ISBN: 979-8-7652-4781-5 (e)

Library of Congress Control Number: 2023923092

Balboa Press rev. date: 12/14/2023

CONTENTS

For
Carol Overing
and
Marilyn Robbins

DISCERNING -

Dear friend
Put no careless faith in these words
For a word miscast
Is an innocent liar
But if image or myth
Strums true on the chords of your heart
Attend, explore
Work to find yourself in its folds
Listen honestly to the dirge
Of your own myth's complaint
Unravel the knot that becomes you
Find the nut of your sad lament
Buried deep in your soul
And mine the treasure
Hidden there

LILIES

Come
Bring lilies of forgiveness
From the gardens of your lives
A gift, a symbol of our innocence
Of judgement set aside

Come
Place the love of lilies
On the altar of our souls
Gaze on their illuminating beauty
Listen to their old, old story
Telling me, telling you, telling us
We are forgiven, beloved, One
Shining in each other's shining eyes
And in the eyes of God

ABOUT THIS BOOK

"Bring Lilies", is a collection of poems arranged to illuminate themes and ideas relevant to spiritual development today. It is a tapestry of words and images. It weaves my own experiences into a map of spiritual clues that point to the treasure we are all seeking and to the realization that we are the "apple of God's eye".

The material is not new. It has been influenced and shaped by the work of many, many others, ancient and modern. For example, readers who are familiar with, "A Course in Miracles" or "The Holy Bible" will recognize their formative influence on these pages. And followers of Erik Erikson, Louise Hay, Carl Jung, Fritz Kunkel, Robert Monroe, Caroline Myss, Eckhart Tolle, Maryanne Williamson and others may also recognize their particular imprint. It also bears the stamp of those wonderful wise ones I know personally.

My friends Carol Overing and Marilyn Robbins, The Women of St. James' Anglican Church Writing Group, my sisters Carol Eydt, Louise Metham, Juanita Taylor and our whole family and so many more have offered support and encouragement all along the way.

Let me say that whatever is good in "Lilies" is given by Spirit and those mentioned above. Whatever is less helpful reflects my own inadequacy in discerning and communicating.

Writing "Lilies" helped me focus on my own spiritual journey in new and rewarding ways. Perhaps it can also add a little light to brighten your path. I hope you enjoy reading "Lilies" as much as I have enjoyed preparing it. Go slowly. Read and reread. It takes repetition and practice to become fluent in looking to Love.

INTRODUCTION

"Bring Lilies" is about transformation. It speaks to the huge benefit of embracing a spiritual journey. It focuses on the excitement of developing an active relationship with the Holy and on the wonder of an emerging higher Self.

"Lilies", makes the point that spiritual attentiveness reconnects us with the reason we agreed to undertake this life. It reminds us that our journey, here, is designed to provide the learning opportunities necessary to our eternal mission. And it helps us see that we create the path we are on, and we choose the differences we make, on a moment to moment basis.

"Bring Lilies" asks us to reflect on the life we are actually living now. It asks us to let all that has gone before fall away into Spirit's hands so we can be clear in the present moment. It is an attempt to uncover the beauty and strength of the human soul and to shine a little more light on the known way.

If "Lilies" has come to your attention, then you are already on the path. If it speaks to you, then wander through its pages. If it is not the path for you, ask Spirit to show you another way. All roads lead back to Love.

CHAPTER ONE: *AWAKENING*

CONTENTS

AWAKENING

CHAPTER ONE

AWAKENING

LISTEN

Listen! Can you hear renewal rising? Is your life vibrating with the one note hum that refreshes all things? Are you riding the tide of a new day dawning? Are you singing the song of the turning wheel?

The whole of slumbering creation is dreaming a new song. Push forward through your silence. Sing and dance into your enlightenment until together we become the humming, flowing, dancing wheel that lifts the new voice up out of inertia and plunges it fresh, into clear streams of living water.

Listen to the universal call for transformation. Open to the path of light.

CALLING

When I was little
I heard someone calling
No one believed me
That frightened me

I escaped to the park
And climbed high up in the pine tree
I swayed with the branches in the breeze
And heard God speaking

There was no Eli
I was not Samuel
I did not say
"Here am I Lord"
God kept calling
Across the years
I kept trying not to hear

I did not believe God had time for me
Or really needed me
I did not really listen
Perhaps I had no time for God

And I still hear God calling
God leaning in with love
Ever more abundant
I know now that
God's love is relentless
And I who am created in God's image
Am relentless too

There is no stopping God
There is no stopping me
There is no stopping you
Together we roll on as One
Reaching ever deeper into Love

AWAKENING

Deep in the soul
The gift, the treasure
Precious and holy
Lies waiting, resting

Cocooned in
Its mummy-case
Hidden away
Protected from
Curios eyes and clumsy fingers
Beyond greedy ego and harsh terrain
Hidden especially from you and me

Deep in the soul
Potential feels Spirit
Hovering, calling over the water
And she gathers and grows and stirs
Till she bursts her container; freed, full-fledged

The tender pale shoot
Powers up
Searching for light
Answering Spirit's call
With her own driving longing
Flailing her way
Through stone and clay

She bathes for an instant
In the moon-lit night
Then the moment she feels the light of day
Potential actualizes and falls away
Disappearing, integrated, forgotten

And in her place
New growth struggles for grounding
And reaches for love

ANSWER

I hear You calling
Holy Mother
I know nothing of You
I am an innocent in the ways of Spirit

I am undone by the power
And the gentle stillness
That attends You
As You wrap Your Love
Around my shoulders

I hear You calling
And although I do not know
What You require of me
Or even who I am
I am answering, "Yes! Yes!"

PATH

The narrow path moves toward you
It finds you and calls you and invites you
To join it

It is a living thing
And when you choose to set out on it
In open-minded innocence
It wraps you in its wonder

It goes before you
Drawing you along
A resonating ribbon, calling
Drawing you along

PRAYER

Holy Spirit
Blessed loving Guide
Teach us to pray

Calm us, soothe us
We are a little bit afraid
To call the name of Holy God
We believe we are not worthy and God is angry

Call daughter, I beg you call
Holy God is waiting
Listening, hoping, praying
You will open to the Light

You are the apple of His eye
He created you
In His own image
He sees you perfect

Hold out your arms to Her
There is nothing to fear
Welcome Her into your heart
As She welcomes you

KALEIDOSCOPE

Take us
Shape, remake us
Mend us, use us
We are Your own
And we are all we have to share
A Kaleidoscope of imperfection
Made beautiful in You

INVASION

Relentless
This energy I call, Spirit
It pounds up and down
The empty rooms of my life
Building beyond my capacity
Threatening to capsize me

I stand at the edge
Staring into space
Hypnotized
Already letting go
My hands slip willingly
I drift out
Swirling beyond
I cannot escape
The throb that pulses in this other
It invades my space
I echo my blind response

I do nothing
Know nothing
Feel in violet

There is only awe
And something other
An energy that draws me
A swaying bridge to God

BRING LILIES

He said
"I'm saving your place for you
You know the way Home
And what is more
You only dream that you have left"

He looked into my eyes
And I saw
Where Truth and Light lie buried
I saw myself shining there
At home in Glory

I heard myself
Humming the ancient one note hymn
And telling the ancient story
Passing it on and on

He held out his hand
"Let's go up to the city
Up to Jerusalem
Into the temple of God"

"I cannot," I replied
"I have nothing to bring"
And he said
"Mother
Bring lilies
From the fields of your soul
From the gardens of your heart"

I said
"God has no need of lilies"
He replied
"Bring lilies
For you and for me"

MY FATHER'S HOUSE

And my spirit
Surged up within me
When she heard him say

"I am preparing a place for you
I am saving your place
Come to me"

And I was brought down by joy
Like the sun in the evening
Shimmering, trembling
Carried away

And he called out again
"Beloved come"

I took the outstretched hand
And the known way rolled out
And suddenly and still
God is everywhere
And together
We open the gate

CHAPTER TWO: *ILLUMINATION*

CONTENTS

ILLUMINATION

CHAPTER TWO

ILLUMINATION

REMEMBERING

The ancients say that when we choose to step out on Spirit's bridge to God, all of Heaven rejoices. And Heaven's joy overflows and washes over us as awe and gratitude rise up in us in answer. And our newly remembered love for God and God's everlasting Love for us sing and dance together illuminating us and the path recovered.

AWE

And suddenly we are filled with awe
And awe stays just out of awareness
Always sublimely present
Until it thunders through
And joy rolls down

ADORATION

Oh God we love You
We bow low before You
We honour You. We glorify You
We stretch out our arms to find You
We bless Your Holy Name
Thank You for loving us

BLESSED HELPERS

Spirit, God's own Joy
And Jesus' anointing
We long for You to touch us
Surge up, drop down, flow in
And on through us to others
More, more and more

Sweet Jesus, brother, friend
Spend time, come talk with us
Expand our learning
Teach us to forgive as you forgive
Share your wisdom and your way
You are the living love of God defined
Thank you for the beauty of your grace
Teach us to live like you

PERFECT AS WE ARE

Holy Mother smile on me
For I am sinless as a newborn babe
I know You will not judge me
For what I did not know I knew
And could not do
For You are All in all and Love

We are all equal
The same and different
Not special; not separate, merged, unique
You and you and you and I and we
Are differing aspects of the same One
The One who is Love
And does not need to judge
To find us
Perfect as we are

I AM

Here in this instant
I am indestructible
A star, a galaxy
A dream come true

I am more than I can know
All I ever need to be
Forever becoming
Now

Now in this perfect moment
I am love rising, falling
Dancing, singing, whole, complete
Giving everything; asking nothing
Receiving everything with gratitude and joy
Here in this instant I am

DANCING

I am dancing

Swaying

Turning, yearning

Falling, floating

Spinning, soaring

I am dancing

Dance Joy!

DANCE JOY

I am dancing
Far beyond this earthy plane
Out beyond our starry sky
Floating past the shores of heaven
Dipping down the galaxies

I am heavy-light with dew
Glowing with a glory-hue
Shining with the love of motion
Turning, swaying, bending, leaping
I am dancing

I am spinning out beyond illusion
Whirling in on all that's real
Flowing, gliding, loving, being
Merging in a Heart that's true
I am dancing

BEHOLDING

Create for us a perfect knowing
Spin out for us the Holy Now
Delay, keep short, the separation
Prolong the ecstasy, the awe

Jesus, you are the blessed name
The essence of our souls' desire
Bless the wonder of beholding
The "I", the "we", the "thou"

WORLD VIEW

The real world
The one that God creates
Is present and available
Here and now and perfect

Not wrapped in time and space
Not altered by the senses
Seen by looking with the heart
Into the world of soul and Spirit

PRESENCE

My presence surrounds you
And moves with you
I go with you everywhere
As you come with Me

Fear not
Do not be dismayed
I love you
I am LOVE
I would not, could not, harm you

Know Me
I am with you
Learn to recognize
My Voice

Lean into the wind
Of My Speaking
Flow out
On the river
Of My Words
For I am Very God

I have called
And you have answered
You have
Given yourself
To Me
I have received you
You are Mine as I am yours
Do not look away

CHAPTER THREE: *ILLUSIONS OF SEPARATION*

CONTENTS

ILLUSIONS OF SEPARATION

CHAPTER THREE

ILLUSIONS OF SEPARATION

ALONE

A nd I lean out too far over the glowing red poppies of almost loving and I fall into the scarlet fairy ring of time already spent: Into the ancient rattle of us against them; Into the fear of scarcity and death. And ego begins to whine and howl and call her darkness to her. And darkness comes and settles over me. And I see myself unworthy, alone and afraid.

BIG BIRTH

And God spoke Big Birth
And afforded us the challenge
Of stepping up out of the crystal sea
Into being new, in a new way
Into being aware; into knowing in God
Potentially free to create
To be friends with the Holy
To plant the lilies of Original Blessing

We experienced, experience still
The gift of Big Birth as hostile, cruel
Holy Mother compressing us; pushing us out
Father God sending us out of the garden
Separation, isolation, danger, fear

We do not see Love's joy
In birthing a home for expanded potential
In preparing new, unimaginable Holy gifts
For the little ones swaddled and wrapped in risk

We read rejection not love
Our dream is of an angry God
Pushing us out of paradise
Love gone mad and who knows why?
A dream so frightful it must be right
And in our fear we step into error and out of Truth
And spin the Original Apple myth

We dream of judgement. It is all our fault. We cast the first sin!
And God who is Just, just has no choice
But to send us away dressed in illusions of shame and guilt
And in our hurt we smash the Original Blessing of Birth
And recast it original sin

We forget the Love that leads to God
And invent the lie that believes in death
And we cry to the Wind, "We are banned. We are damned
We can't go home to Eden again. The lilies are wrong"
And all the while through our chatter and fuss
We are safe at Home in the arms of Love

HIDING PLACE

We believe our myth
It is our fault. We disobey
And guilt and fear rise up
As God comes walking through the garden
Calling, searching, loving
Closer, closer, calling

We are guilty, terrified
There is no place to hide
No time, no space, to cover us
No death, to snatch us up
We call in vain for thought to save us
And Fear rises in response
He slithers through the rushes
As time and space descend

He scoops up matter from the air
And draws out limbs and shapes
Every hollow, every curve
Every strand and bone and hair
Sculpted by his touch

"Step in," he says. "I will hide you
Safe from God; away from Spirit"
And the breath of his stale breath
Breaths our first sigh
And it is done

We see ourselves alone enfleshed
Apart from God
As death's illusion
Flutters down
To claim us

BODY DREAM

Body is illusion
A hologram of beauty
A prayer to our inventiveness
A vision, not a cause
The servant, not the mistress
Limited by time and space
Each cell dancing in its place
Completing its circle
In the circles of its sisters
Freely giving, freely taking
Sharing all with all

Body is benign
Not sin, not love
Life's temporary housing
A hymn to separation
A fantasy, a dream
Like a star, a universe, a poem

BODY WISDOM

Wisdom says
Body is receiver, processor
Benign transmitter
Energy field, attractor
A vehicle for sharing
Perfect innocence
With two potential mistresses
She responds to ego
Out of fear of time and death
With shadowy misperception
And futile preoccupation

Or she sees clearly
With compassion's truth-filled eyes
In any given moment
One, not both
It is for us to choose

BODY WISDOM continued

Wisdom says
Care for your body
It is wondrously made
A vehicle for your becoming
A helpmate longing to know soul
A product of your own imagining
Beauty in motion

Dance it fearlessly
Enjoy it fully. Use it entirely
Embrace all it has to teach you
And step up transformed

Wisdom says
Body is means, not cause, not goal
An energy being
Capable of reaching
Well beyond the limits
We assign it

Wisdom says
Body is chemistry in motion
A silent librarian
Sorting, storing, referencing
All she sees against all she saw
She tells what is through the lens of was
Just as we have trained her

Listen to body's own earthy wisdom
Vast truths are written in her heart
Ancient memories sing along her sinews
Creative strength lives in her bones

Do not attach yourself
To bones and flesh and skin
Your body is more, much more
Than what your mirror shows you
And you in God are more again
Eve's child forgives. Love lets illusion go

EVE RISING

And Eve rose
She shook out her long dark hair
And climbed up out of the river
Her body gleamed
She had floated downstream
Much further than she had intended
But the water rippling over her naked body
Was so perfect

She felt wonderful
Then suddenly she sighed
A familiar heaviness settled around her
Adam would be looking for her
Adam the innocent farmer
Adam the unquestioning servant
Adam made in God's likeness
Adam beloved of God

Adam

He wastes his great wisdom

His towering strength

On tilling a garden

And calling creatures into being

Never bothering about the morning

Never considering the evening

Never questioning divine commandment

Never curious about the Holy's motivation

Always rushing to do God's bidding

Ignoring the luscious apple on the tree

Never listening to me

Me? Adam named me, Eve

I am bone excised from Adam's clay

I am separate from Adam, and different

I have the courage to spit in the wind

To shoot the whole bolt

To dance with the serpent

To shake the tree

EVE RISING continued

The serpent is cunning, I know
He says Adam and I will not die
If we eat of the apple
We will be Gods
Knowing right from wrong
Whatever that means?

As for me
I just want to say, "No thank you God
I am my own person; just like You
Separate, independent, worthy of respect
I have rights and entitlements
I will not leave the fruit of that tree alone
Until I have Adam for my own
I intend to taste and see"

I am unsure about Adam: Adam never says, "No!"
He is too busy doing the bidding
Husbanding Eden, by day
And walking with God in the evening
God's man! I am just along
Perhaps if I tempt him

As for me
When it comes to God
I am the helpmate, the companion
Just a bit player, after all
If it wasn't for serpent stirring the rushes
I might never have realized
But now!

What is death, anyway?
What is, "surely die?"
When God said "Do not eat of the tree"
What did that really mean?

EVE RISING continued

Did God say, "No!" to us?
Did I say, "No!" to God?
I think I am afraid
Or was it really all the serpent?
I think it was the serpent!
Yes, it was the serpent
The serpent made me do it

And she said
"Perhaps I made it up
Why would I make it up?
What is making up?"

And she named the serpent, Projection
And the naming of him
Brought him into being
And her fear kept him by her side
Ever eager to do her bidding

He called the sky, heaven
And she dreamed God was there
"Out of sight
Out of mind
Out of heart"
Was what she never thought

As she dreamed
The serpent smiled
And slithered closer
His undulating coils obscuring her view

And she dreamed
She and Adam fled far from Home
She could not hear Love calling
For the serpent's rattle chattering in her ears
She and Adam hiding, running in the dark
Alone together, alone

CHAPTER FOUR: *RELATIONSHIPS*

CONTENTS

RELATIONSHIPS

CHAPTER FOUR

RELATIONSHIPS

JOINING

We are created Love. Love is our essential nature. It is joyful and inclusive and shares out of its abundance. We frighten ourselves with dreams of independence. We imagine we can distance ourselves from the unity of everlasting communion and still feel safe and happy: And we set out to find love on our own terms.

We slip out of our higher Selves through the heavy door of ego-mind into the way of the world, in search of a separate identity and "love out there". We experiment with power-over and declarations of unworthiness. And eventually we come to see that we cannot find peace and happiness by ourselves. When we begin to explore the potential of God's gift of relationships, with forgiveness and love we see the little gap that leads to the way back Home.

GAP

The holy spark of automatic knowing
Defines the gap
The space for change
Where learning waits
In Spirit's hands

When we share the path together
"Then" becomes "now"
And the now of then is known
For the first time, now

Then, the little spark of learning leaps
Igniting Truth, freeing, forgiving
Loving, healing, growing
In the timeless dance
That is our golden blessed task

HELP US TO LOVE

Holy One
Help us to love
As Jesus loves

Draw us away from
Self-centred relationships
Into the blessing of loving
Love pressed down and overflowing

We are not able without You
We do not see Love as You see it
Show us the secret of innocent
Unconditional, everlasting Love

LOVE?

What is love? How do I love?
Can I really love you?
Do I love you for myself?
Am I driven to seek you out?

Is my hymn to you
An ode to an addiction
Buried in the pages of the past
And triggered now
By a semblance of what was
A glance, a phrase, a mannerism?

Is my love for you exclusive?
Does it shut others out?
Am I destitute without you?
Can this be love?

How do I love you?
Do I love you for yourself?
Am I attracted to you by Grace?
Is my hymn to you and yours to me
An ode to joy for all the world to share?

Is love released now
By the echo of an ancient Holy love
Humming the joy
That tunes the spheres?

Does the thought of you bring peace
Asking nothing, needing nothing
Offering all, receiving all?
Can this be love?

TOGETHERNESS

"Can I see God alone?"
"Only in part
And part is illusion
God is Truth
And Truth is whole"

"Can we see God together
In gatherings of two or more?"
"We see God by seeking God
In each other, in ourselves
And in the universe

We see God
In inclusion and affirmation
By laying down
Our desire for independence
And embracing
The Oneness of togetherness

We see God
By pondering the collective
Below the surface
And by guiding it
Up through shadow into light

We are equal, not special
The same and yet unique
Loved equally, loved completely
Loved just as we are
Beloved
Together we see God"

MY DEAREST ENEMY

It has been so long since
We clanged together
Differences unfurled
Banging our tin cups on our highchair trays
Rattling our empty worlds
Spitting hateful slurs
Snarling projections
Attacking mindlessly left and right

Scratching, pinching, biting
Kicking, pulling hair
Anything, anything to hurt and hurt
And hurt again

I have missed
The stockade fence conversations
I once relished in your absence
Alone in the night chattering to myself
Planning brilliant repartee

Uncovering, exploring unique options
Defending my every action, each idea
As if it were my flesh and blood
And you were here and out to cut it down

I hated you with passion
I loathed you, wished you dead
I would have choked you
But I couldn't stand to get that near
I laid traps for you. I tripped you up
And buried you alive, as you did me

We met together
No holds barred on no man's land
Where friends and lovers never venture
We knew each other's every fiber
Denied the good, enhanced the bad
And sold each other's tattered reputation
To anyone around

MY DEAREST ENEMY _{continued}

We fought, we lost, we learned
And suddenly you slipped away
And left me bruised and torn

And now I never sleep
I search the boundaries of my life
Mounted in full armor
In the heat of the noonday sun
For fear you might suddenly reappear
To steal away my upper hand, my right, my confidence

I wish you'd come, again
I learned so much from you
My dearest enemy
You showed me who I am
And how far I have to travel
I love you more than you can know
I forgive you all you never did
And pray you do the same for me

SPIRIT FRIEND

Can I respond to You?
Can I catch You?
Can I stand free before You?
No reason, no cause, no expectation
Soul-naked, confident, trusting, loving?

Can I grab fate from Your hands
And let meaning soar?
Can I fan the spark of reflection
And hold truth in awareness?
Can I release the all-consuming violet flame
Of You and I in present being
Spiraling into One?

FRIENDS

Two circles
Dancing life
For love of Holy God

Between them
The silver chord
Of friendship

The magnetic field
Of, "Gathered in my Name"
Charged poles, placed just so
Creating tension, energy
Transforming out of time
Forgiving, loving, healing
Calling one to all
And all to One

HOLY FRIENDSHIP

What is a holy friendship?
It is a gift from God
A timeless thing, a holy now
A vehicle that moves us
Passed the past
By bringing what was fearful into the light of trust

Syndromes, clusters
From the past that hold us back
Are remembered
And emerge to be re-lived in dialogue today
And corrected out of time here in the now

As each unhappy pattern falls away
Shared light rushes up to take its place
And friends and friendships grow in grace as darkness falls
away
And Spirit sings a bright new hymn to friendship and to
God

LEAP

Two strangers went a strolling
Around the park one day
They talked about their journey
Along life's bumpy way
They walked a little faster
To be fit was the goal you see
They talked about the face of God
And wanting to be free

Two women dragged
Around the damp park's bends
They shared the gloom of shadow
Each hoping for a friend
They walked a little straighter
Health was the goal you see
They talked about the Love of God
And pondered Calvary

Two friends faltered
In the park's dark gloom
The Way was cold, the snow was deep
The climb to Heaven, steep
They ploughed on with resolution
To be whole is the goal you see
They say their prayers and share their doubts
And ask for grace to see

Two seekers stride
Around the park's green bends
The Son of God flies on ahead
Calling out their names
He laughs and talks and takes their hands
And draws them in his wake
Forgiving, blessing, sharing
Faster, faster
At the edge they do not pause
They hold Christ fast and leap

SOUL-QUEST

"Holy God
Can we know our own souls?
Feel the one note hum
Strum the silver chord
Singing death to ego
Singing life to love evermore?"

"Together you can
Your separated self
Believes you are alone
And vulnerable
Fear flits along
Your thought lines
It shoots out from your bones
Coils in your gut and muscles
And sings your sad and anxious song

Take the hand of a friend
Walk with Spirit between you
Pray for the grace to discern
Feel for the tug. Listen for the hum
Soul is present all through the day
Making herself busy, helping
Through any medium, in any kind of way
Calling you, telling you, loving you

Pause, listen. Take time
To discover each other and God within
Friendship building openness
Openness uncovering what has been hidden
Truths revealed strengthening souls
Soul strength transforming friendship
Soul friends transforming friends and enemies alike
Loving friends extending God
God extending friendship, expanding souls
Love growing Love"

UNFETTERED

Do not name me
Let me be free to be myself
Do not see me from your memory's eye
Let me live unfettered in your mind
Myself, as I am meant to be

Do not judge me against your standards
Nor make of me a caricature of your own invention
A fantasy you share with others
Out of mind and without thought of consequence

I do not exist in your snapshot album
I am my own illusion
And behind that fearful dream
My truth runs free

Dear friend please help me find
My own true Self

ACCEPTANCE

Let us deal gently with our ignorance
Our waywardness
The moments when we leap
And hold the gain
The times we slide back into pettiness

Weaknesses, strengths, triggers
Let us accept all of them
As belonging to the circle
Creating our togetherness
Permitting our learning, authoring our growth

It makes no difference where they originate
It only matters that we do not attend them
Give them strength, make them real
It only matters that we open to understanding
And fear gives way to love

CHAPTER FIVE: *DOUBTS AND QUESTIONS ALONG THE WAY*

CONTENTS

DOUBTS AND QUESTIONS ALONG THE WAY

DOUBTS AND QUESTIONS ALONG THE WAY

FORGETTING

Deep inside we know that we are spiritual beings and love is all we need. However, as we move more completely into forgiving relationships and give more of ourselves to Spirit, ego becomes anxious.

Ego is consumed with concern for its own survival. It realizes that as we grow in grace it loses control. It prompts us to forget God's love by painting the Divine in vengeful and capricious hues. It takes steps to prove that our natural loving nature is weak and a liability. It tries to distract us from our life plan and our journey by holding itself up as our only reliable saviour. Ego demands that we remember judgement and forget Love. It raises doubts and questions at every turn.

DOUBTS AND QUESTIONS

I step
Out of the journey
To pause at the manger
And ponder my life
Questions and doubts
Assail me

What is life?
Why was I born?
What is my purpose in being?
What am I carrying into the world?
What am I nurturing under my heart?

Where is my faith
My hope, my peace?
Why do I feel so unworthy
So anxious and guilty?
Do You care about me?
Have You really chosen me?

Are You pleased with me?
Are You listening to me?
Why don't You answer me?

What is the meaning of the universe?
What is this journey of planets and stars
And the whole earth family?
Where are we going?
What are we doing?
What is Your purpose, Your plan?

Is there really everlasting life?
What is my soul?
What is my body for?
Is there really a God?
Is it You?

WHAT IS ABUNDANCE?

Holy Mother
What is abundance?
What is light?
What is love?

How can we move
From fear of abandonment
To a platform of abundance and gratitude?

And once there
How can we move from a position of abundance
To love for the neighbour who hates us
And on to the Glory of God within?

How can we forgive
Those with more than us
Help those who abuse us
Love those who refuse us
Holy One, what shall we write?

Daughters write this
"God is light
There is no darkness in God
Everything is in God. Everything is God
God is complete
There is nothing apart from God

God is abundant Love
More than enough for everything
All love comes from God
There is nothing outside of Love
Only the illusion of illusions

Anxious ego stands apart from love
Throwing stones, digging traps
Loving soul leans into God, into abundance
Beloved, have faith. Put your questions aside
Truth is real. All will be clarified."

CREATION OR COINCIDENCE?

Random or planned?

Evolved or begotten?

Man-made or Spirit-attracted?

Science or religion? Religion or science?

What is truth?

What is Your Wisdom, Mother?

What shall we write?

"Daughters write this

And the ascended

Stand trembling before Me

In agonizing Love, brought down in Joy

Waiting, pleading

To leave their illusions behind

And step up out of substance

To transform and sink deep into Love

According to My desire

Religion and science
Both are human constructs
With the capacity to help
As long as they are conceived in
And guided by Love
They are means not ends

In ego's self-centered hands
Religion and science
Are driven by greed and desire for control
Grim taskmasters spiraling down
Dragging you into futility

If you have ears to hear
Then choose or deny religion and science
According to the attraction of Love
If you have eyes to see
Then forgive and illuminate
Whatever Love places before you"

MARY OR MARTHA

And in the night
An angel came to me
And I dreamed
And in the morning
A voice spoke into my heart
And said
"Write!"
And I knew
That I would write
The ideas swimming in my mind
Unformed bits unconceived
Through Advent, Christmas and Epiphany

And I answered
"I will write
But first let me sweep the kitchen
Fill the dishwasher, start the wash"

And the Voice replied
"Daughter, why must I come last?
Why do other needs come first?
Why must the work of God
Wait in the wings till all is done
And your illusionary time has fled?"

And so, I write
Not knowing what I write
Praying that the holy muse attends me
Worrying about what others think
As I sit typing
With the house all awry
And the garden calling

Trying to ignore Martha's heart
And turn from inner criticism
And shadow's strident chatter
As Mary did

PARADOX

The love of God so rich and fair!
Who is this god that kills Egyptian infants
In a fit of vengeance
And spares his chosen people
In a burst of unconditional love?
Are we not all one and all beloved?

Who is this god who claims I live forever
And calls out, "Dust to dust"
To my sealed coffin's face?
And gathers little children to his breast
Then lays them broken in the grave?
Can this be the Loving Source of life?

These questions haunt me
As I stumble through the scandal of my faith
Where is my help?

HEARTBEAT

Holy Mother God
What is our Heart of hearts?
Who sets its rhythm?
Who hears its song?
Where does it beat?

Is it "I" in the morning?
Is it "we" in the evening?
Is it one of us? All of us?
Who is our heart?

"Daughters, there is one heart
Beating out one rhythm
Resonating all in All
This Sacred Heart is shared
And beats in everything
It contains the Christ-light
And the potential of all things
Open to becoming"

CHAPTER SIX: *GOD'S SCHOOL*

CONTENTS

GOD'S SCHOOL

CHAPTER SIX

GOD'S SCHOOL

WILLINGNESS

When we are young in spirit Holy Mother feeds, guides and encourages us with joy and synchronicity. It is a blessed time of orientation and illumination.

As we grow in grace Spirit draws us away to the mountain and shows us the illumination that flows from the heart of God. And we come to see that while we can know nothing in and of ourselves, all knowledge and understanding are available to us if we are willing to learn to open to Spirit's gentle teaching with patience and innocence.

LEARN TO RETURN

Beloved
In order to return to Love
In order to be complete
And happy
We must be born again

Born anew
To the blessings of childhood
To natural curiosity, and open hearted-innocence
To sweet vulnerability, and a willingness to trust
To risk, to forgive, to believe

We need to unlearn
To uncover, to recall, to remember
The essential loving-Self
That is the holy gift
We are born with
Our true Self, strong and free

In order to attract us
Back to Ourselves
The Holy, gifts us
With a distant, compelling memory
Of Love everlasting
Of our ancient perfection
And the Home we never left

And Mother surrounds us
With loving guides and teachers
Who, like Spirit, never leave us
And with learning opportunities
And peak and valley experiences
Repeated all along the way
Until at last we become them

Take heart, say yes, step up
Light the little lamp of learning
Prepared especially for you

GOD'S SCHOOL

Today in this moment
I speak in the voice and language
Of the Pod
The one voice we all
Finally speak into and out of

Today I come to greet you
As Myself
Beyond body
Beyond time and space
Loving, fantastic, powerful
Incorporating the voices of many

In this view
I bring you greetings from
The halls of heaven glowing within you
We say to you

Do not mistake your task
You have come
Desiring to embrace learning
You do not come recognizing that you are complete
And on a magic carpet of entitlement
What would be the point in that?

You come to master illusion, forgiveness, freedom
You come anticipating the learning challenges
You agreed to on the other side
You come desiring to struggle
To learn to live the graces
That extend the pod and Heaven

We thank you
We greet you with the kiss of welcome
We bless you as you take your place in God's school

RECEIVE

Meditate
With the intention of discerning
Embrace opportunities as they arise

Pray
Seize the moment and step up
God is pleased with you
Beyond your knowing

Beloved
Learn to choose God
All else is given

BRIDGE

It takes two or more to make a gap
And God
To make the silver chord
That guides the holy journey

A chord spun from
Holy potential, given opportunity
Tiny incremental choices
And a simple constant discipline
Choose to find Christ in one another
And in yourself

Learn to hold the tension at the synapse
Be present in the still point of the vortex
As Holy Impulse leaps to close the gap
Spirit's gentle swaying bridge to God
That draws us into newness

TEACHER

Love within forgiveness
Flowing flowing
God is One
And One is all unchanging

Patterns dark
At first unseen but then emerging
Within, without, integral, interlocking
Holy Spirit my soul's beloved teacher
Welcome, Come
I draw You to me
Draw me to You

LEARNING AND TEACHING

Listen to Spirit

Learn to discern

Sometimes I am the one to ask

And you are the one to answer

Sometimes you are the one to ponder

And I am the one to know

It does not matter

Learning and teaching are one

As we are one

Only listen and ponder together

Discern as One

CLASSROOM AFTER CLASSROOM

We pause in the road
Lost in pondering
Life and death and afterlife

The penny drops
Our eyes snap open
Misperception falls away
As Vision powers in

And we see
We know, for a moment
That we are mistaking
This finite, little life on earth
This wonderful Spirit-attracted learning opportunity
For our unimaginable everlasting perfect Selves

We are astonished
By the simple revelation
That what we call "death"
Is simply graduation
Followed by a rest, a break
A summer holiday
A study week
At Home in God

Then back to school again
In a new classroom
Or perhaps a new assignment
In another dimension

GRADUATION

When a course is finished
The student does not die
The learning is assimilated
And the candidate steps up or down
Into new learning or new work

And the details of
The course completed
Fade and fade and fall away
Threads of memory
Disappearing
Into the living fabric of a life
A distant echo
Eclipsed in the excitement
Of a new day dawning

EXTRATERRESTRIALS

We come to earth
To learn, to teach, to share the news
That the Love of God
Is everywhere
And all there is
Is Truth and Joy expanding

Classroom after classroom
Life after life
Will pass away
But you and I in God remain
Forever Home
Forever perfect as we are

GUIDES AND WITNESSES

In truth
I am without history
Without future
I am timeless
I am Now

In truth
My perfection is lost to me
In a sea of misperception
I am blind to my reality
Caught in the twilight of illusion

I am the complaint
And the complainer
I contain the answer
And the question
But I cannot see myself

Who will walk with me
And show me
The fantasies I call memories
The dream I call myself?

Where is my human witness
My friend along the way
The guide who milks my truth
And feeds it back to me
That I may know?

Come Spirit
Come guides and witnesses
Come friends and enemies
Help me
Offer me Love
And it will return to you
Pressed down and overflowing
Where is the help I need?

CHAPTER SEVEN: *ILLUSIONS OF DUALITY*

CONTENTS

ILLUSIONS OF DUALITY

CHAPTER SEVEN

ILLUSIONS OF DUALITY

CONUNDRUM

In those moments when we are aware that we are Love, we look for ways to extend Love. The world we see then, and the choices we make, reflect the bliss we are living. In those moments when we believe the illusion that God has moved away from us, we see ourselves as vulnerable and alone. The world we see then and the choices we make reflect our submission to the laws of ego-mind and to the anxiety and hostility they create.

Love lifts us above ego and loosens its control over us. Ego responds by fabricating myriads of dualities and contradictions. It tries to convince us that it is imperative that we immerse ourselves in the futility of judging and choosing among them; and in establishing laws and rules to protect our sense of right. It does this to show us that: We are separate; Love is irresponsible; Forgiveness is weak and dangerous; And attack not Love is the only viable option.

DUALITY

There is one path
With two views
On the right heaven glows
On the left the neon attraction
Of the material world blinks frantically

Each is calling us
To live from its perspective
On the right, our Higher Self
Calls us to blessing
On the left our frightened ego
Calls us to futility

The reality of unity
Is our seamless peace and joy
The illusion of separation
Drives us to fear and judgement
We select one not both in any given moment

Eventually
We will choose one
Almost exclusively
As the other slips away

Heaven or judgement?
Which do we choose
Here in this moment
On this the first day?

Look to Heaven
Step up into forgiveness
And duality fades
Into Love

PROOF OF THE PUDDING

I say
"Global warming
Is the major danger of our time
Management of the environment
Is crucial to the future of our children
Lifestyles must change
Immediately!"

And yet I drive a car
When I could walk
I choose what is cheaper
Rather than what is local

I do not learn enough
To vote responsibly
I use cleaning products
That are hostile to the environment

I turn a blind eye
To the dust and dirt
In the corners of hospital washrooms
I follow my own desires and ignore the collective good

But surely
I am not the major danger of our time!

These evils that I see
They cannot be assigned to me
I will find their causes out there
And complain and agitate
Until they are put right!

And I limp along
All mired in guilt
And shrouded in a dying world
Choosing my greedy self
And blaming others for my sins

THE FLOCK

We come to the garden
Late in the evening
We know the way ahead is difficult
And full of tears and pain
For the lonely, burdened shepherd
And the milling, bleating flock

"Will you pray with me?"
The holy one asks the beloved, faithful
"Can you help me through the night?
I need to feel your love, your strength"
"We will!" they answer glibly
And quietly fall asleep

They feel let down
He isn't what they thought he was
And they are tired
After all it's very late

Our priest stands before us
"Can you help me through this day?
I am so alone and in despair
Will you support me with your prayer?"
And all of heaven leans out
To the bemused and fussing flock
With blessings for their anointed one
"Of course!" is our reply

Do we watch with her and pray?
Or do we sheepishly turn away?
Do we bring him down in tears
With unkind gossip, winks and slurs
Diminishing the Kingdom, ourselves and Mother Church
It isn't that we judge. After all we love her very much
It's just that he is not what we expected
We are so very busy
It is late and we are tired

BLIND SPOTS

We were at table
She said, "I hate politicians
I can't stand politics

Seemingly good people get elected
And what do they do?
After a year or two
They exploit their office
To feather their nest

They cow-tow to big corporations
And prostitute their election promises
In order to increase their control
And the likelihood of being re-elected
They seem blind to what they are doing"

And you said
"You focus your discontent
On other people, in this case, on politicians
But what if you were the only person?
What if you are really all there is?

Close your eyes
And draw those imagined others
Into yourself
Imagine you are both yourself and the politician
Imagine you are yourself and the CEO
Both the imagined good person
And the one you are finding fault with

Now that you are both
Now that you have the power and the opportunity
And the temptations, limitations, demands and threats
Will things be different?
Can you look to God and multiply abundance
Can you step above duality?
Can you be Love?"

TWO ASPECTS OF SIMON

And they sent Peter down
To lay hands on the newly baptized
And Spirit filled them and claimed them
Peter the Holy Man

He did not need personal power
Holy Spirit powered him
He did not need recognition
He was regarded by God
He did not need to entertain
God shone through him attracting others

There was another Simon
A magician, an intuitive who played to the crowd
He needed personal power
Desired adulation, wanted glory
He performed, to be seen to be the Son of God
In truth, he was the child of God as we all are
And did not know it

Simon the magician
Heard the word
He wanted to believe
But he did not open to innocence
He was baptized but did not empty

He saw Spirit heal through Peter's hands
And thought to buy the gift
Of spreading God like a magician's cloak
And wrapping himself in stardom

Oh Simon Peter, pray for Simon
Do not judge him
Forgive your brother for his folly
He cannot choose one master. He tries to cling to both
Forget his greed, his jealousy, his fear
Love him back to Love
And walk with him rejoicing

MY WAY

He carried
His priceless treasure
In an old leather bag
Made shiny with use

It was his, reflecting him
Made for him by Holy God
To hold the precious seed
Seed for the wine, the bread
The very life of all that is

His was a human soul
Strong, beautiful, reflecting God
Carrying the seed, the potential
The very Word of Very God under his heart
Words, seeds scattered by his hand
On every kind of ground

There was another
Who carried a treasure
Born on the wind of mind
Swept up in myth
Fragmented by ages
Distorted by cultures
Deceptively simple

It was his, reflecting him
Given to him in a holy dream
He was a human soul
Strong beautiful, reflecting Christ
God in everyone. Everyone in God
And the vision he shared was
Reflected, projected, refined, distorted
By every kind of listener

MY WAY _{continued}

And they came
By separate paths
To the foot of the cross
They came bickering, jostling
Demeaning each other

Peter the Rock
With the seed in the sack
And John with his dream
Mutating the seed

"I am right" each cried
"Did God not choose me?
Am I not special
Beloved of Christ
One of a kind
One set apart?"

And the philosopher dreamer
Threw his laser of scorn
At the old leather sack
And the humbled seed spilled
At the foot of the rock
Spoiled by doubt
And human misperception

And there at the cross
The Rock
Smashed his sword down
On the mind of the hand
That defiled his old leather bag

The seed on the wind
Could not be reclaimed
By the mind that dreamed it
It was scattered and spoiled
By the law of the blade

MY WAY _{continued}

And both were bereft
Frightened and angry
And the one hanging there
Looked down
And sighing asked

"The seed in the pouch
What is its fruit?
The word on the wind of the mind
What is its harvest?
What is the treasure you each hold so close?"

And they cried as one
"The treasure is love, Holy Love
Love of God; Love of neighbour
Love of friend and enemy alike
To love your neighbour as yourself
To do good to those who hate you
Love is the treasure, the pearl without price!"

And they bristled
And shoved and threatened
And took up the sword
In the name of the Lord

To protect and defend
The Seed from the Word
And the Word from the Seed
To kill and to maim again and again

And Jesus closed his eyes and turned his head
"Father forgive them"
Was all he said, and he blessed them
And his love and forgiveness roll on and on
Down the centuries, over the years
Sending us out with the Seed and the Word
Reclaiming us from duality time after time
Bringing us Home to Love

CHAPTER EIGHT:
TRANSFORMATION

CONTENTS

TRANSFORMATION

CHAPTER EIGHT

TRANSFORMATION

CREATORS

We have said that we are climbing the path from ego-mind to higher Self: And that Spirit is the co-designer of our journey and our constant loving guide and teacher. The terrain we are scaling is our own life, and our progress depends on our willingness to participate in a journey of personal transformation.

Our role is to stay awake; scan; listen for the Holy and bring what we experience into awareness for exploration. We are asked to forgive, and to forgo judgment based on memory in favour of unveiling what is. We are asked to meditate, pray, study, ponder and discuss with loving friends. We are asked to be open to the journeys of strangers and to serve in community. As we begin to let our self-serving, fear-driven patterns go and embrace the inner light we are transformed and we become new.

REVEILLE

I was bored
Thought life was winding down
Asked God to help me be more loving
To thaw my cold, cold heart

I was full and emptied
Depression stalked
My tattered soul went searching
Out along the reefs
And left me lonely
Caught in a life devoid of meaning

In dribs and drabs, I heard
The wakeup call
"Help others, don't reject them
Find shadow, learn to dream and dialogue
The way is hard but so exciting
Begin beloved; Begin now"

PAUSE

The holy place
The timeless moment
Enfolding, emptying, purifying
The little Light, the violet Fire
Transforming, transmuting

Alone, we are but waiting
Frozen, in a dream of death
Unable to call, to run, to flee
From the darkness billowing up
Around us

Spirit, name us, claim us
Fill us with your cascading power
Create the still-point within
Show us the innocent Christ
Grant us the freedom of One

SHIFT

I thought I saw sin one night
I was waiting for Phyllis
She was at confession
It was Lent and the holy artefacts and symbols
Were draped in deepest purple
My young soul was shocked
At the feeling of dark depth there in the sanctuary

Suddenly I thought I understood
That sin was squirming
Under each of those drapings
My sin, the wrongs I believed I had done
Tiny vicious vipers
Whispering to me
Trying to get me
To own them, to focus on them
So they can possess me
And change me to their liking

I reached out
"Yes" I said
To the Stations of the Cross
"Sin is hard at work
I smell it
I feel its tentacles
Reaching out to claim me"
I shrank back
I whispered "sorry"

And then I thought again
I remembered God is All in All
And Good. There is no sin in God
I was wrong and my belief shifted
The only sin there is
Is the illusion I choose
To give space to

SIN

When I honour ego
And turn my back on God
I choose conflict, not love
I chose out of fear, out of greed
Out of desire for approval, out of pride
I chose for me; for something other than love

And the pebble that is the illusion of sin
Falls into the reflecting pool
It splashes and the ripples circle out forever
Capsizing my baby's little boat
Sinking the leaf with the ladybug's eggs
And the tears role down

And with the dawn I see that it is I who choose
I choose to turn away and mire myself in darkness
I choose to withhold the lilies of forgiveness from myself
And I reach out to choose again

LEGION

In the beginning
I saw myself, one, separate
Then they tumbled out unbidden

As we walked and talked
And were distracted
With thoughts of God and wholeness
Ego slipped them through unnoticed

There, in the gap, each makes a presence known
They do not ask permission
They merely take their turn upon the stage
Confounding us with their remarks
Their power to disassemble

As they move about firing triggers without warning
The defences of our strongholds shatter
Our weakness is exposed and we are sore afraid
And growing in grace

ARK FOR A COVENANT

Somewhere
In no place
There lives a mythical ark
A living, breathing, container-home
For all that finally, really attracts me
Really draws me
Out beyond the horizon of my understanding
In search of Holy God

It is frail like iron
Ethereal and thick as weathered leather
It is light and beautiful
And darker than a dungeon

Left to itself it is a wild thing
Caught up in contradictions
Torn by inner tensions, inflamed by passions
Overwhelmed by storms and storming

It cannot name and does not understand
The milieu, the culture I have created
It simply carries the potential
The full-blown blueprint of my Self
The whole, potentially complete
And the memory of Love and Home

In its clearest moments
My soul is totally attuned
To Heaven's call
And to remembering who I truly am
In God

HOLY RECALL

Memories of Heaven's perfection
Create my soul's trajectory
Heaven's holy draw
Enlivens my soul's single-minded passion
To forgive
And return to Love

I forgive the dream
Of my alienation
I forgive myself
For dreaming it

I give thanks
That no matter how tangled
My journey may seem
In realty
I am at Home in God

CONFUSION AT EVERY TURN

Holy one
Save us from this confusion
From the polarization
The duality
That confronts us at every turn

Shape us
Guide us
Use us
Help us to transform
To become all we really are
As your will requires

INTERCESSION

I prayed
And as I prayed
I thought I heard a crack
It wasn't loud
It split the room
Illusion broke asunder

The darkly glass
Flashed crystal clear
The lying mirror shattered
My face lay glittering on the floor
Shards of self, fragmenting

I prayed again
My prayer resuming
Again the crack and then again
Louder than before

Fetter after bondage snapped
My unmoored life
Sprang free of dream and metaphor
My soul lay raw and gasping
Unclaimed upon the floor

The slow dissolution of my life
The terror of the melting ice
The beauty and confusion
Of the still small voice
Beating about my head
So quiet it was screaming

"Hear Me daughter
Daughter, please attend Me
Step up out of illusion
Guess not, to not know
Spin your pseudo truths no more
You are finally ascending

INTERCESSION continued

Cast the magic web
To the four winds
And turn away"

I prayed and
Silence deepened
The crystal tomb exploded
The razor crystals slithered down
And scraped me free of dreaming

I prayed and
Silence deepened into God
Awe washed through
And left me new
And shaken

SISTERS

Above all else
When you come to the crossroads
And the direction is unmarked
And dark distress settles over you
Pause in silence

Call to Spirit, to help you
Study your own life's myth
Take Spirit's hand and the hand of a friend
Go in and down
And up and back
All through the dark, dark night
Searching, listening, pondering
Uncovering, waiting, sharing, forgiving

Until the little light of learning
Descends
Revealing the known way

WAY STATIONS

The womb is temporary
A place of becoming
Do not cling to her past time
Do not run back to her
To hide yourself in darkness
To escape from challenge
Do not avoid her
When transformation is upon you

ON THE CUSP

When a transformation
Nears completion
And you have nearly resurrected

There comes a time
When time and space
Become too small for being
And dread descends
With hope in hand

Then time is short
Quiet yourself
Explore your new dimensions
Prepare your heart
For the most difficult of journeys
The journey of leaving
What you never were
And leaning into what you are becoming

ON THE CUSP continued

Do not struggle
Walk the inner path
Of quiet contemplation
Like the infant on her carry-board
Learning to stretch her tiny soul
Her body quiet

Like the full-formed moth
In her tight cocoon
Mind-dancing tiny stretches
Preparing, strengthening
Unexpected wings
For unimagined flight

The old pattern is almost gone
And cannot be recalled
Do not regret it
Learn to become the risen you

Lose no potential talent
Because of fear
Gather willingness
To make the leap
Faith will teach us how to fly
The new born you with a broader view
A vision of lilies and sky
And rock and grass and leaf

Pause now
Stretching, drying, fluttering
Then fly; gliding, soaring
Sharing life with all you meet
In a new way

SHADOW HAWK HAWK SHADOW

In the North, in the red oak
In the sunny frigid cold
The ruffled hawk sits
With her back to me
Calling me to attend her

"Be aware, sister: Be aware
You cannot escape me
I am waiting un-entangled
You know I am your totem
What happens to me happens to you
No matter where we are located"

In the frozen south
The great hawk rises
And the shadow of her passing
Sees my self's own shadow overlaid in hers
Mine locked rigid in the ice-cold depths
Her's locked diving down the steel-grey sky

Her call loosens my recall
I struggle to answer
Swaying free of the bits and pieces
That hold us bound apart
Together, out of all awareness
Swaying to the same unheard siren's shriek

She plunges over me
Slowly I rise
Serpentining up among old drowned branches
Until I reach the frozen sky
Eyes huge, lungs bursting, fingers clawing ice

SHADOW HAWK HAWK SHADOW

continued

"You cannot come to me"
She screams as she dives by
"As long as you lie buried in that frozen crypt
And I cannot pull up to save myself
Until you come to me

Look away from death, look away
Look to life in God, like Jesus
Look and see and save us all
I look, and in one fell swoop
We slam together Whole"

PHANTOM

Are you your inner person?
Your God ordained Self?
Or are you a fragment
A mask, a persona?

Find the real You
Know your hidden heart
See the Kingdom longing for you
Feel God's Love leaning out
Hoping, waiting, knocking

Answer with yearning
Take time for learning
Bow down in joy
And let the mask go

HELPER

I dreamed of a bird
Red, white, and black
With the greenest
Insect dangling from her beak

She was perched on
A pale, ceramic mosque
And there, under her talon
Lay Holy Mother church

The bird nested
Inside the window of
A dirty, whitewashed, cobwebbed cellar
Her chicks around about her
The fledglings contented
The bird contained
The church impaled

I dreamed
You opened the cellar window
With a gift of lilies for me
And potential freedom
For mother bird

My heart froze in terror
If she should fly and be unable to return
The gift is death for the unfledged flock
For loss of her

It was the safety of the children
The status quo I choose
Not the lilies of forgiveness
Not freedom for the mother and the church
I caught her gently as she rose to soar
And started down to put her back
Thinking to save the little flock
By imprisoning her
And I became confused
And lost my way

LAST CHAPTER

What can I say
That will release
Your hold on your illusions of tomorrow?
What can I show you
That will distract you from the past?

What can I offer
That will unfold the miracle of now
The joy of presence to you?

Look into the garden
See the juncos flitting
White tails flashing
Under the berry trees
Fluttering together
Glad to be home in Dundas

See the burning bush
Orange berries glowing
Under fiery red leaves
See the crimson cardinal
Flashing a bright orange beak
As he selects among the seeds

Is the bush not beautiful?
And the birds and trees?
Does God not walk in the garden
Here and now?

When you are preoccupied
With things that are over
If you focus
On dreams of things to come
If you overlook the beauty right at hand
You choose to miss the blessing wholly present
And forfeit the wonder that you are
Beloved, choose "now"

BELOVED

What can I say to convince you
That you are beloved of God
That God is pleased with you
And cares for you
Without alteration
Just as you are?

How can I persuade you
That the Holy wants you to love Her
Of your own initiative
As you are here and now
God did not call out "Prodigal"
To the mythical youth
We did that!
God threw open His arms and heart
And welcomed the wanderer Home

SPIRIT TALK

What can I say to you
About the peace that is already yours
Tucked away under all the chatter
You throw up to drown me out?

Can you hear me?
Can you listen?
Can you step aside from
Driving yourself to distraction?

Can you pause?
Can you turn your phone off?
Can you keep your fingers still
Long enough to focus
On this one thought?
You are Love, and precious beyond all knowing

Step up out of judgement and duality
Be who you really are

YOU SHALL COME REJOICING

How glad God will be
When you step up out of self-doubt
Away from guilt
And throw off unworthiness

When you
Hold out your arms to Spirit
And step into Love
Forgiving, forgiven, free

How glad God will be
When you are the song
That sounds across heaven
When a seeker returns

How glad you will be
When you come to the crossroads and choose Heaven
And Love carries you Home rejoicing

AT HOME TOGETHER

Teach us to forgive
Instead of judging
Save us from insisting
That we are unworthy
Help us to include and to affirm

Help us walk gracefully
Across the waters of unknowing
Firm in the knowledge
That we are Your temple
And You are within

One, together at Home
In the temple
Of our Sacred Heart
The light of the world

CHAPTER NINE: *TEMPLE*

CONTENTS

TEMPLE

CHAPTER NINE

TEMPLE

RETURNING

Some say we are the temple of the living God. That our soul is the home of the Holy and our heart the sacred inner sanctuary. They say that we are co-creators with the Divine and if we are to participate fully, we need to prepare by opening to Spirit and walking within. All that is required of us is a willingness to step up out of ego-mind into innocence.

Ancient writings teach that our inner temple is protected from us as long as we are fearful and self-centered. They teach that God is always present, and waiting for us to choose to return to the Love that is Unity. And when we set out on the return path it is Spirit that guides us Home to our Self and the altar within.

BODY REVISITED

Jesus
Overcame ego and body
His body was buried in a tomb
His ego never was

And yet he is here in the midst of us
Showing us
That the material world
Is commanded by life
And in fact we never die

He puts a perceivable body
On and off as he wishes
He materializes and disappears
According to our needs

He did not aspire
To power over others
To material possessions
Or to self-centeredness
Of any kind

He knows compassion and sharing
And moves in Love
Distributing all that is to all
As Spirit leads him

His soul is the temple
Of the Living God
And deep within
The inner temple of his soul
Rests his compassionate, sacred heart
We also are the temple of the Living God
With the capacity to love, and to restore
Body and Spirit

MERGER

My soul is ethereal

It has no obvious existence in the manifest

Though it makes its presence known

It is not a dream

It is the essential me

My soul has always been

And always will be

And although it is perfection

It seeks to learn, here, in the linear

According to God's plan

My soul longs

To extend heavenly knowing

By experiencing the physical that body knows

Soul wants to see and hear and feel

To touch the earth and pick a flower

To hold an infant newly born

And body extends to help her

My soul in turn
Expands body's range
By offering opportunities
Designed to help body
Risk the comfort of the known way
In exchange for presence
In peak experiences
Like forgiving, sharing, loving
Joy and peace and hope

Body and soul, earth and heaven
All exploring the margins, playing the fringes
Merging, integrating, exchanging, extending
Helping each other into One
Shaping the plasticity called life

TEMPLE

And I went up out of the glaring sunlight
Of an empty city street
Up across the threshold of a mighty church
Into shafts of shade

Large blocks of natural stone
Shaped its soft sunlit porch
And along the side, flying-buttresses
Formed tall triangles
Secret shadowy spaces

Light-dark places
Places to talk unheard
Of things sacred and profane
Faith, doubt, temptation
Secrets from all but God
Unwise, perhaps; but still

I entered
Through the ornate door
And stepped into beauty
Suspended in space
Splendour in white and gold
A vault so high that sound rings back
And falls like snow on silence

A great stone wave rolls on its side
Along the huge rear wall
Concave, convex, concave
Liquid marble swirls the altar
Streaming out to greet the east
And in the moment
Blessed silence
Melts the noonday heat

A group enters behind me
Chatting, laughing
Spilling down the aisles

TEMPLE: continued

Peppering the dark pews
With expectant, bobbing, colour
Stirring up a breeze, a swirling, pregnant, little wind

A pause, a hush, an undulating silence
As eyes sweep up
To unveil the pulpit
Riding high among the statues
Under the great banners

At first nothing
Then a quiet resonating hum
A simple chant
A different kind of loving
Flowing down over the altar
Eddying out around the pews
Whispering as it comes
Embracing as it passes
Telling and telling and telling us
We are perfect and God is Love

BAPTISM RENEWED

Is your soul covered over
Hidden from help?
Rescue her
Let the water of life-everlasting flow in

God's living, healing water
Pray it down from above
Draw it up from below
Pour it out for your sisters

Dance in it, splash, wade out
Swim the Joy of the Lord to the rhythm of God
And your soul will rise up
Like the sun at dawning
Lose yourself. Sing

INNER SANCTUARY

Toward evening
I paused in the secret shadowy place
Between the buttresses
To listen to the message
I stood there among the men
Praying for ears to hear

I paused in the shadow
To ponder the meaning
Of the seemingly heavy-handed church
Beautiful, holy and yet confining

And as I pondered
My gaze lit on a little door
Tucked away from careless eyes
In the shadows
It opened to my hand

And I went down the chiselled steps
Behind the great stone wall
Into a lower, rounder, dimmer, older space
Filled with softly glowing lamp light
A second sanctuary, tucked away
In tapestries and velvet hangings
Old style paintings, fragile statuary
Delicate carved olive and rosewood panels
A gentler touch made by smaller, but still strong hands

And there
Below the pulpit, before the altar
A beautiful woman was speaking
Speaking of this Jesus and his message
Showing him to me and me to him
In a woman's voice with a woman's eye
I smiled. She smiled. He smiled
And my heart made ready a sacred room
Tucked away from a casual eye

WILD THING

My soul
Is the temple of the Living God
She is the container of my potential
She holds the outline of my life plan
All my essences and holy attractors arise in her
She is a wild thing, anxious for nothing
Totally in love with God

SOUL TALK

My soul speaks a language
All her own
She is not impressed with my idea of logic
Or our culture's laws and preferences
She is feather-light
And drapes around my shoulders
Like a wrap
Or glides on ahead
Skipping and humming
To herself

Joy and love attract her
She is naturally curious and unpredictable
Capable of attracting the dark side
When her potential is ignored
Much given to mystery
And what I call mysticism

SOUL TALK _{continued}

My soul knows truths
And shares them with me
She tells me things that apply in the moment
So I can use them
And pass them on to others

When I ask for her advice
On matters of dualism and justice
She takes my hand
And draws me up and up and back and back
Until the world is small and blue and beautiful
And all there is; and together we gaze on it
And the polarized issues
Collapse in and fade away
And earth shines bluer
As soul hums her happy song to God
And smiles mischievously at me

She whispers
"Lovely, dear, lovely"
As I scramble for balance
Between inner and outer
Knowing somewhere deep inside
That God is All and all is God and Good
And my loving soul is blest and blessing me

EVENSONG

I asked to see
And I closed my eyes
To ride the waves of sound
Rising, falling, swirling
In the early evening
Near the closing of the day

I asked to see
And I closed my ears
To bathe in the billowing light
I saw clouds of indigo
Rising, swirling, fading, merging
With silver-shot turquoise
And sunset pink
All on a summer eve
Near the closing of the day

EVERMORE

And do we speak of
Life and evermore
Yes, we speak of futures
Yet unseen
Beyond the bend ahead

And when your hand
Slips from mine
And your eyes close
As you go forth, unfettered
What shall I wish you?

I wish you beauty
I wish you joy
I wish you truth
I wish you the glory
Of the face of God
Welcoming you home

CHAPTER TEN: *LILIES*

CONTENTS

LILIES

CHAPTER TEN

LILIES

GETTING TO LOVE

C hoosing to act for love illuminates us. Old ways, old desires fall away. New values and ways of being emerge. We are not what we were. We become new, born again. Our approach to ourselves and to others is more open-minded and inclusive. We replace judgement with forgiveness and compassion. And these changes are reflected in the thoughts and responses we send out into the world and beyond.

The love that we send out comes back to clarify our vision and gift us with new dimensions of understanding. It supports us as we step up through the fragrant arms of the lilies of forgiveness into the light of the wise indigo night. It dances with us in the wild violet fire high on the mountain of grace.

GRACES

Holy Mother, thank You for
The gentle gift of gratitude
That calls me to open to my senses
To let all preconceived assumptions fall away
And to rejoice
In the beauty of what is

Thank You
For the feel of early morning mist
So gentle on my cheeks
And for the fluff of Truffles
Purring back and forth around my feet
For the evening sounds of mockingbirds
In love with love and little ones
And little ones in love with food and life

Thank You
For the quiet glow of fireflies
Flicking on and off along the dark hedge row
For racoons coming by at dusk
To steal a bite to warm the evening chill
And share their darling children
With the woman down the hill
And for the moonflowers' glow on indigo
In the soft September night

For these
And for the gentle breezes
Carrying the fragrances
Of late summer in their arms
I offer heart-felt gratitude and praise

MOVING DAY

I am moving
I am moving back to Graceland
Into the home prepared for me so long ago
My new home is spacious, bright and full of joy and peace

High ceilings, crystal windows
Large, fragrant, woodsy rooms
Walls of translucent amethyst and alabaster
Furniture of pungent cedar beautifully crafted
A symphony of textures, a harmony of colours
To lift my spirit and extend my soul

My new heart's vision sings the glory of the view
Oh the beauty and abundance of the gardens and the fields
The wild river's song and the music of the spheres
My Home is ready, the carpenter is calling
My soul is longing, there is no need to wait
I am moving as we speak

VISION

The joy of music
Underneath my heart and in my ears
As I am walking in the park
Soars me, turns me, remembers me

Suddenly I feel Your presence very near
And I begin to pray

The horizon shifts
The escarpment ridge is redefined
The sense of depth grows vastly deep
And the trees so crisp and green
In clarity and definition
Stand free and clear against the sky
And joy fans out and back

THIS LITTLE LIGHT

And in a moment
Of suffocating bondage
The illuminating light of Moses'
One God
Draws us aside and speaks

We did not expect
The flaring fire of
An illuminating God
Burning in a bush
Untamable, unquenchable, non-consuming
Burning in and through all things
Burning from within the source

That great flame ignited our hearts
And eclipsed the surface flickers
Of a thousand squabbling lesser lights
The hierarchy of masks competing for our souls

We turned our backs
On all we believed we knew
We reached out to the flame
We saw ourselves unworthy
And we pulled back from Holy Ground
Adrift, separate
Unable to forgive
Shunned by God
Or so we believed, and family

Isolated points
Of hidden light
Dimmed by shadow
Rapt in darkness
Standing silent, paralyzed
Accusing ourselves
Behind the iron veil
Waiting, praying, straining
Searching the night sky for who knew what

THIS LITTLE LIGHT _{continued}

We have heard
That one is coming
A king born into the Jews
A sun born out of
Moses' own One God's
Unimaginable Love
A Prince of Peace
One bringing
Love, compassion, healing, joy

It is foretold
That he comes
In Spirit's shadow
Heralded by angels
Announced by the light
Of a new star
We would welcome his arrival

And all unknowing
Synchronized as one
We focus our desire
On our frosty breath
And pour our energy
Into our hearts
Willing the space for the song
And the gap for the light
Willing Spirit to teach us
Forgiveness and
Love for ourselves

We stand
Alone and yet together
Each on a distant hillock
All in the bleak midwinter
Calling angels
Giving thanks for a new star
Peering inward into indigo
Praying for a perfect song

THIS LITTLE LIGHT <small>continued</small>

Longing for a different
Point of light
Dying to see ourselves
Shining beloved
In God's shining eyes

And suddenly
Three distant strangers
Cast in one plot by all that is Holy
Hear as one
A world changing crack
Like a splintering shard
And the tiniest trill of brilliant sound
"Hallelujah, glory, glory, hallelujah"

And the sound roles through
The choir that sings the earth
From its very foundation
"Joy to the world"

And three
See as one
A tiny crack
And a sprinkle of sparkle
Growing, glowing, shining, calling
Casting its light up from under the sand
New to our eyes

And the new ray pours up
Drawing us down, calling us inward
Showing the way
Through rocks and shoals
And treacherous rivers
Till the light stands still at the edge
Illuminating the place
Behind the iron gate
Beyond the great stone wall
And together we come to the brink

THIS LITTLE LIGHT <small>continued</small>

And we who are love
Stoop low at the mouth
Of the interior cave
We step in without pausing
And the huge dark stones
And locked wooden gates
Barring the path
Melt like mist
As we pass, unhindered
And we glide through the indigo space
As a song and a star burst forth
Full-fledged

And there at the center
Before our wondering eyes
Is the inner light
All soft and round and glowing

Innocent love

Love, beloved, loving

The new promise of power

Potential and glory

And for the first time

We see

That we are the mother of God

Chosen by heaven to carry the flame

Our soul is His temple

Our heart Her sanctuary

She is the light of our life

Our reason for being

We bend over the manger

Wrapped in a whisper of angel wings

And welcome the little One up

We gather Her to us

All splashed in Her halos

And wreathed in Her smiles

THIS LITTLE LIGHT <small>continued</small>

We hold Him high
In the starry night
Trailing all that ever was
And She shines the light of love
Baby wise

And God's own great ray
Gentles down into Hers and ours
And together we carry Him on and on

For we arc the light
Bringing hope to darkness
Illuminating what is not seen
Bringing secrets to truth
Bringing Love to the world

SHINING EYES

Forgive, affirm
Bless your sister and your brother
Hold your enemy dear

Affirmation brings
The joy of God to heart and mind
And freedom comes to light awhile
When we see that we are One
Shining in each other's
Shining eyes

PODCAST

We rise together
In response to who knows what
Casting ourselves on shafts of air
Real and imagined

Ascending
Lifting as one
Wheeling, circling
Turning, in the afternoon sun
Hundreds of points of sparkling light
Sharing the same secret name

Glittering
Like moon beams on water
We wheel and circle and bank
Attuned

We careen over wheat fields
Sailing like snowbirds
Abandonment mothering skill
Togetherness building joy

Souls inseparable
Trajectories merging
Knowing, known, forgiving, forgiven
Forever extending
Loving in harmony

Galaxies of souls
Adoring Rejoicing
The Pod coming Home
Flying fearless in God

FOURTH WISEONE

And tonight
He steps
Beyond the shadow of the cross
Out from the gates of hell
Away from the stillness of the tomb
Into a soft spring Easter morning
Full of angel light
And Holy love

And tomorrow
He comes new
Through the shadows of the years
A gentle man
A humble God
Offering His hard-earned gifts of
Lilies, Love, and indestructible life

On a soft spring morning
He lays these treasures down beside
Gold and frankincense and myrrh
At the manger of our new birth
And smiles into our upturned faces
With shining eyes

EPILOGUE

Thank you for accompanying me on the "Bring Lilies" journey. I hope you enjoyed reading "Lilies" as much as I enjoyed preparing it. I must leave off writing for a little while. I have reached a crossroads and new words have not yet come. I know the way ahead will be challenging but also full of hope and joy. And I wish you God's speed as the path unfolds.

I believe that more people than we can count realize that the gift of lilies is the way to peace and love. I believe there are millions of people like us in every corner of the world who are struggling to throw off illusions and uncover the inner light. And I believe that a critical mass is building rapidly and dawn is at hand.

In the meantime - The blessing of the Lilies and radical forgiveness will lead you home.

> *"Therefore, if you are offering your gift at the altar and there remember that your brother has something against you, leave your gift there in front of the altar. First go and be reconciled to your brother; then come and offer your gift." Matthew 5.23-24, NIV*

Printed in the United States
by Baker & Taylor Publisher Services